The Practice of Joy

Insights from the Tales of C S Lewis

Andy Swinford
Educator and Retreat Leader

GROVE BOOKS LIMITED
RIDLEY HALL RD CAMBRIDGE CB3 9HU

Contents

1 Leading with Joy 3

2 Joy Together 7

3 Creation Joy 13

4 The Invitation to Joy 20

Notes 27

Acknowledgments

Grateful thanks to Tom Benyon and Ian Silk for their encouragement in the writing of this text.

First Impression May 2024

ISSN 0262-799X

ISBN 978 1 78827 389 3

1

Leading with Joy

Too much of life today is joyless. Young people despair of a future and a hope, unable to get on the property ladder, their planet compromised, food banks a normalized part of life, graphic scenes of war on our screens. We live fearful for the future and conscious of extreme suffering in the world. The Christian joy is needed now as much as ever it was.

The good news is still good and therefore joyous. Read Mark or Luke for a sense of how Jesus led so much of the time not with anger but with joy.

C S Lewis too leads with joy. He wrote an autobiography of the years up to his conversion, aged 30, based around the concept of joy, saying 'In a sense the central story of my life is about nothing else.'[1] It is small wonder then that the subject pops up repeatedly across the broad sweep of his work. It can be found just about anywhere, including, and perhaps especially, in his fiction. The stories reveal Lewis's insights into the matter in a way no academic exposition ever could.

They have brought me joy from an early age—taken to the public library every Wednesday after school by my mother, I repeatedly wanted to borrow just one book: *The Lion, the Witch and the Wardrobe*. It was through Lewis I encountered a particular variety of joy: a delight, an abandon, a lightness, like a song.

It is a quality of joy that is often overlooked, which crosses paths with holiness, beauty, and the deep, deep goodness of God the Father. It has the loveliness and sweetness of springtime about it. It is waiting to be rediscovered in the writing of C S Lewis.

I found much later in life that the *Chronicles of Narnia*, and Lewis's other fiction, can be read as devotional material. Page after page of these stories rewards our close attention and can move us to self-examination, prayer and, yes, rejoicing. They invite us to open out rather than curve in on ourselves, to share joy.

Our Duty and our Joy

Aged 17, Lewis discovered the fantasy novella *Phantastes* by the Victorian writer George MacDonald on a bookstall at Leatherhead train station—on his way home from a haircut, of all things. It is a story he described as, on one momentous evening, 'baptizing' his imagination. He said the 'wind of joy' blew through it.[2] Looking back much later from his Christian perspective, he defined that quality as holiness. For Lewis the holiness and the joy are interconnected. It is my belief that his own tales of Narnia, and of other worlds too, also carry the presence of God.

Lewis described a particular form of the joy in his autobiography *Surprised by Joy*, a spontaneous delight which contained at its heart a pang of longing, a quite painful yearning. It always pointed further off, and could not be pinned down as an end in itself. It is very different from mere pleasure or happiness or intellectual and aesthetic satisfaction, he said. Aside from his extended consideration of this particular experience, he does not provide us with a systematic treatment of it in its many other manifestations, but it is possible nevertheless to discern a robust spirituality of joy in his writing.

Lewis often comments on joy as a Christian virtue in his correspondence. On St Paul's instruction to 'rejoice in the Lord always' (Phil 4.4) he says we should try our best to obey, and that one of our commonest sins is to neglect doing so. Lewis was in the habit of making three resolutions every morning and trying to obey this command was one of them, he wrote to his friend and former pupil, the Benedictine monk Dom Bede Griffiths.[3]

I believe we can make ourselves vulnerable to joy

It may be that joy cannot always be produced on demand, but I believe we can make ourselves vulnerable to joy. We need to be somewhat intentional about it. It is a practice, something to be learned, to be grown in. Lewis sees it almost as a duty, as he says in another letter to Griffiths: 'We must, if it so happens, give our lives for others: but even while we're doing it, I think we're meant to enjoy our Lord and, in him, our friends, our food, our sleep, our jokes, and the birds' song and the frosty sunrise.'[4] He frequently refers to the joy to be had in such everyday things.

The joy is often mediated for Lewis by nature, an aspect very important in the light of our contemporary concerns about environment and climate. After all, the Bible starts with God standing back and looking with joy upon his creation. One of the saddest journeys of the Bible is the one which Adam and Eve make out from Eden, away from the immediate presence of the God of all joy.

As a retired English teacher, alongside leading retreats and online classes about C S Lewis I have more time for outdoor things like gardening, walking and beekeeping, and I have learned with Lewis's help to appreciate more deeply the joy of the creation. Lewis has the ability in his writings to help us attune our ears once again to the sound of the Lord God walking in the garden in the evening breeze (Gen 3.8).

These are healing stories—leaves for the healing of the culture (Rev 22.2), sweeter than honey, and the drippings of the honeycomb (Ps 19.10). How may we then extract this healing?

No Settled Happiness

I have often heard Christians make a distinction between a superficial happiness which comes and goes with our surface mood, and a lasting deep-down joy in Christ. Lewis does not overtly make this distinction. What he does say in *Surprised by Joy*, and repeatedly so, is that in his own experience there was 'general happiness' once, as a child in his Belfast home, which was lost for ever upon the death of his mother when he was nine, but that nevertheless throughout life 'There was to be much fun, many pleasures, many stabs of joy.'[5]

In *The Problem of Pain* he makes this into a general principle: 'The settled happiness and security which we all desire, God withholds from us by the very nature of the world: but fun, pleasure, and merriment, he has scattered broadcast.'[6] He argues that if we were permanently happy we would be tempted not to bother with God, not to fight the things which get in the way of our spiritual growth. All the same, we are allowed plenty of joys along the way, because occasional fun, enjoyment and even ecstasies will not carry the same risk. Accordingly, joy, pleasure and merriment all feature large in Lewis's writings.

When his wife Joy was bedridden with cancer, he told his friend the writer Dorothy L Sayers, 'We have much gaiety and even some happiness. Indeed, the situation is not easy to describe. My heart is breaking and I was never so happy before: at any rate there is more in life than I knew about.'[7]

With the death of both my mother and brother in 2020—the year of COVID-19—I have felt some affinity with Lewis in his sorrow. Even though I had heard all my life about the deep-down joy of the Christian faith, it was still with some astonishment that I often experienced, amid great sadness, a virtually simultaneous joy.

If we should not expect settled happiness in this life, what can we expect?

In the memoir *A Grief Observed* Lewis tells how he had always warned himself 'not to reckon on worldly happiness' and is shaken by his inability to trust God through the pain of loss in the months after his wife died, yet he speaks with wonder of the times of happiness and even gaiety that he shared with her even in the darkness of her final illness.[8] If we should not expect settled happiness in this life, what can we expect? How can we learn to find joy in everyday things? How do we train ourselves to notice God's joyous creativity burgeoning around us? How can we contribute to the fulness of joy of our communities? These are some of the questions raised by Lewis's treatment of the matter. Lewis is at pains in *Surprised by Joy* to explain that, in the end, the joy he describes points beyond itself. It is ultimately a pointer to Christ. How might we access this joy?

In the Narnia tales it is Aslan himself who so often brings joy. Think of the delight of Mr and Mrs Beaver in telling Lucy, Susan, Edmund and Peter that Aslan is present in Narnia and 'on the move.' Or the great joy of the romp of Lucy, Susan and the lion on the hilltop at dawn when Aslan is risen in *The Lion, the Witch and the Wardrobe*. So it is with Christ. He is the great joy-bringer. I believe it is his voice, his presence that we desire more than anything.

When the lion departs at the end of *The Horse and His Boy*, we are told, 'There was a short silence and then they all stirred and looked at one another as if they were waking from sleep. Aslan was gone. But there was a brightness in the air and on the grass, and a joy in their hearts, which assured them that he had been no dream.'[9] Like Christ, he always leaves joy in his wake.

Joy-gathering

- As we set out on this adventure of joy, what memories of joy stand out from your past?
- What are your initial ideas on how you might make yourself vulnerable to joy?

2

Joy Together

Lewis's fiction has brought home to me (an introvert), that joy is frequently a shared joy. It is a grace given us by God which finds its summit in community. That does not necessarily mean a large crowd of people. It might just be one other person. When Jesus prays in John's gospel for his companions and followers, he desires 'that they may have my joy made complete in themselves' (John 17.13 NRSV—the footnote offers also '*among* themselves'), and the context suggests that his joy attains its fullest expression, its completion, in the togetherness of God's people, in their unity with each other and with God.

We often see this 'joy made complete' in the *Chronicles of Narnia*. For example, in *The Lion, the Witch and the Wardrobe* some of the earliest companions sent to the children as they play their part in defeating the evil White Witch are Mr and Mrs Beaver, with their steadfast loyalty to Aslan and his purposes. The chapter devoted to the dinner at their house is a delight. The kettle is singing, the frying pan hissing, the marmalade roll steaming and the pot of tea at the ready or, for Mr Beaver, the mug of beer and a pipe—all just as Lewis enjoyed it, and the company of six around the dinner table, unpretentious and down-to-earth.

It is something of an antidote to the privation of the Witch's evil enchanted winter, the cold and the snow and the darkness safely outside. After the meal each one leaned back and 'gave a long sigh of contentment.'[10] At the Beavers' cosy home the meal, including all their talk of Aslan's coming, is like an act of defiance in the middle of what is, after all, a story of war against a formidable enemy.

In Time of War

We too are at war. We should perhaps think more intentionally of our own mealtimes with friends as acts of battle in the struggle against evil and despair in the world, or the glad gatherings of our fellowships as celebrations of Christ's conquest over death and darkness. My church in Birmingham often has meals after Sunday services outside on the terrace, which is a public space, in part as a joyous witness to, and incarnational participation in, local community. Household mealtimes too are worth fighting for, time spent together in the presence of 'the unseen guest,' a stand for solidarity and celebration in a world which tends to pull us apart.

Edmund did not enjoy the dinner with the Beavers. He had been hoping for rooms full of Turkish Delight, which is what the Witch had promised him. When she first gave it him, he had instantly developed a craving for it. But indulgence does not lead to joy. His face was flushed and he felt sick, yet still he wanted more. And now at the Beavers' even the pleasure of food, which is a gift from God, is tainted, his palate jaded. Lewis spells out the principle for us: 'There's nothing that spoils the taste of good ordinary food half as much as the memory of bad magic food.'[11] In blunt terms the indulgences of darkness diminish us and distort our perceptions of what is true, good, and beautiful.

Edmund slinks out of the room, recalling the departure of Judas from the Last Supper, both bent on betrayal. In turn, this draws our attention to a last-supper element in this meal. Earlier they had all been working together very happily in the preparatory chores: the girls help Mrs Beaver cut the bread, while Peter helps Mr Beaver catch the fish. We are not told what Edmund was doing. Presumably just sulking in a corner. The freshly killed trout is not exactly equivalent to the bread of the eucharist, but it may remind us of the feeding of the 5000, a miracle which John in his gospel places just before Christ's declaration, 'I am the living bread that came down from heaven. Whoever eats of this bread will live forever; and the bread that I will give for the life of the world is my flesh' (John 6.51).

The scene with the Beavers is in deep contrast with the succeeding episode which shows the treacherous Edmund arriving, alone, at the Witch's house where the hospitality leaves much to be desired. The hard bread and cold water he gets are more like the prison food of traditional fairy tales. There is no Turkish Delight after all, and certainly no joy.

The meals of shared joy in the Chronicles are often celebrations of new-found freedom

The meals of shared joy in the *Chronicles* are often celebrations of new-found freedom. In *Prince Caspian* the enemy has been defeated with the help of the awakened trees, and in one crazy scene the trees dance (yes, dance) a feast into existence which is so extraordinary it takes more than a page to describe. It is 'a magic dance of plenty.'[12] This is free Narnia restored, full of joy, wildness and deep gladness—and high-end provender! Afterwards they all nod off to sleep by the fire with good friends all round. The physical circle of friends, be it round the Beavers' dinner table or around the campfire, is a common motif. In his autobiography Lewis declared, 'Friendship has been by far the chief source of my happiness.'[13] I look back with great satisfaction on the roll call of companions God has sent me in my own life, some just for a short season, some for much longer periods, as the children in the story might have looked back on the two Beavers and Mr Tumnus—and always enjoying food together.

Redemption

We can learn a good deal about turning outward from ourselves and entering into the selfless joy of truly Christian community by considering the character of Eustace in *The Voyage of the Dawn Treader*. It is not a war story this time but a quest for long-lost knights and, ultimately, Aslan's country, or heaven itself. Eustace is the unwilling and downright nasty companion of Edmund and Lucy when they are drawn into their third Narnian adventure. When people comment on his case they usually focus on his redemption, a baptismal scene in a high mountain garden, performed by Aslan, who acts like Christ in our world, but there is more to be drawn from the character of Eustace.

The Narnian part of the story begins with the joyous reunion between Lucy, Edmund and their old friends on the deck of the *Dawn Treader*, most notably Caspian and Reepicheep the mouse. In a chapter of *The Screwtape Letters* given over to the subject of laughter, devil Screwtape identifies one of laughter's chief causes as sheer 'joy,' and his example is the heightened delight seen among friends who reunite with great affection just before a holiday, laughing at their own bad jokes. This mode of joy is similar, Screwtape says with distaste, to the joy which can be found in heaven. We will see it at its height in the reunions in the 'heaven' of *The Last Battle*, climax of the Narnia series.

This heavenly warmth, then, on board the *Dawn Treader*, is spoilt by one person: Eustace. He strikes a sour, sulking note, and very soon makes a bitter enemy of Reepicheep, the noble mouse who will stand for no such nonsense. What with the charm of the ship, the glory of the sunset sky and the thought of discovering unknown lands at the edge of the world, Lucy 'felt that she was almost too happy to speak,'[14] but this is in sharp contrast with Eustace's unhappy and mean-spirited diary entry which follows, in which he self-centredly gripes about his cousins, the ship, Reepicheep, King Caspian and everything ('He might see that I shall be ill if I'm kept in that *hole* any longer').[15]

Eustace has no joy other than the pleasures of resentment

After a near-catastrophic storm the ship limps to an island where work on its repair begins. Eustace isolates himself physically when he makes off into the mountains, with the purpose of avoiding work. He has no joy other than what Lewis calls elsewhere the pleasures of resentment. His descent into the hell of himself is paralleled by his fall into a hot and lifeless valley, where he creeps into a dead dragon's lair. Full of dragonish thoughts, he becomes himself a dragon.

By grace it turns out for his redemption. In his isolation he realizes he no longer wants to get his own back on others. He longs for ordinary human friendship, for talk and laughter, but now he is cut off from all that for ever. In his terrible loneliness he gathers some insight into himself, and weeps. He learns, essentially, one of the chief lessons of living in community—it is not all about me. There is joy to be had in being kind to others. It is something we are all constantly having to relearn. Read in the light that there is something of Eustace in all of us, this story is deeply challenging.

Remarkably, still in his dragon form, Eustace is initiated into the joy of helping others. He flies in meat for them, and a pine tree to make a new mast for the ship. He creates fire and heat with his breath. He takes some of them for rides on his back, to survey the terrain. 'The pleasure (quite new to him) of being liked and, still more, of liking other people, was what kept Eustace from despair.'[16] There is reconciliation between him and his former enemy Reepicheep, and a great friendship grows between them. After an encounter with Aslan who frees him from enchantment, we are told, 'Great was the rejoicing when…the restored Eustace walked into the breakfast circle round the camp fire.'[17]

Here again is the joy of companions gathered in a meal-circle, welcoming Eustace back as a friend, despite his former obnoxiousness. Helped by the compassion and empathy of his cousin Edmund, entering into that circle to join the breakfasting symbolically represents a happy restoration to community. It parallels the person whom Jesus urges to get reconciled with the brother or sister who has something against them before offering their gift at the altar (Matt 5.23–4), a precursor to Paul's vision of the communion table as a place characterized by peace amongst God's people (1 Corinthians 11).

Breakfast is such an ordinary meal. Here it marks a new start, the mercy that is new every morning, for Eustace. When he laughs, it is 'a different laugh from any Edmund had heard him give before.'[18] We are not told in what way it is different. Previously Eustace' idea of a good laugh was to swing Reepicheep round in mid-air by the tail. Now I like to think his laughter was free from malice, marked by a delight in all goodness, born of a purity of joy.

Feasting at the Edge of Heaven

In a letter responding to a question from a 10-year-old reader Lewis explained that *The Voyage of the Dawn Treader* was chiefly about 'the spiritual life (especially in Reepicheep),' a comment which invites us to read with our focus on the growth of its characters, several of whom have spiritual journeys to navigate.[19] It is illuminating to re-read it in this light.

The voyage has been pretty unmagical until the endragoning story, and the meals likewise. All the food that has been mentioned previously were the dull and limited rations on board ship. As things get more magical so do the meals. On the magician Coriakin's island there is a comic scene in which invisible Dufflepuds bouncing in on their one foot bring soup to the table (well, some of it!). Then there is the three-course lunch Coriakin produces for Lucy at his magic table, conjured out of nothing. Notably, Coriakin himself 'drank only wine and ate only bread,' a clear eucharistic reference.[20] But it is on Ramandu's island, close to Aslan's country at the edge of the world, that a more magical, if not mystical, banquet is prepared for the travellers.

It is an evening of untold loveliness, under strange new stars which Lucy studies 'with a mixture of joy and fear.' They arrive at dusk at the table spread with exotic meats and pies and fruits. The fragrance of the fruit and wine blows towards them 'like a promise of all happiness.'[21] Ramandu's daughter tells Lucy that their island is called by some the world's end and that the magical banqueting table on the flagstoned platform surrounded by pillars has been provided by Aslan for anyone who journeys this far. It is Aslan's table. In its proximity to Aslan's country, it is a foretaste of heaven's banquet, a sign of the unimaginable provision the creator has prepared for all his people.

This is the most dreamlike of all the islands they have visited since Narnia, brimming with magic and sacredness and a hint of danger. The joy in these chapters is a kind of wondering holy excitement. When Ramandu the ancient star and his daughter sing their 'early morning kind of song' as the day dawns and the sun rises above the sea, bigger and brighter than normal, Edmund reckoned it was the most exciting moment of the whole trip, not the fight with the sea-serpent or the endragoning of Eustace, because now they realized they were near the world's end, so close to Aslan's country, and therefore to the lion himself.

The knife clearly defines the meal as eucharistic

At the centre of the banqueting table on Ramandu's island lies a long stone knife, a holy and awful relic. It is the knife once used by the White Witch to slay Aslan back in *The Lion, the Witch and the Wardrobe*. This clearly defines the meal as eucharistic, linking it to the death of Aslan, and through him to Christ's crucifixion. The knife occupies a similar function to a cross on the altar at communion. The feast itself is magically replenished every sunset with exotic and lovely foods, reminding us of the perpetual sustenance offered by Jesus to his disciples, the bread which satisfies eternally. When Ramandu's daughter said on the first night, 'Why do you not eat and drink?' it could be the voice of Christ calling to the world. 'O taste and see that the Lord is good' said the Old Testament songwriter (Ps 34.8).

The notion of the feast which is so close to Aslan's country, or to heaven, inevitably reminds us of the wedding banquet and rejoicing in heaven announced in Revelation, and the beatitude spoken by the angel: 'Blessed are those who are invited to the marriage supper of the Lamb' (Rev 19.9). Feasting proclaims the great Christian hope and the marvellous reunion in heaven.

It also reminds me of the extraordinary episode in Exodus when Moses and seventy of the elders of Israel, halfway up Mount Sinai, gaze into heaven and see God, with sapphire pavement about his feet, and under divine protection 'they beheld God, and they ate and drank' (Exod 24.11). They too, very close to heaven, feast.

In a way, the most miraculous meal in *The Voyage of the Dawn Treader* is the simple one provided at the end by Aslan, appearing in the form of a lamb—fish roasted over a fire on the shore at the uttermost fringe of the world. The lamb says 'Come and have breakfast' and is meant, Lewis confirms in a letter, to remind us of Jesus on the shore of Galilee after the resurrection: 'At the v. edge of the Narnian world Aslan begins to appear more like Christ as He is known in this world. Hence, the lamb. Hence, the breakfast—like at the end of John's Gospel.'[22] And 'it was the most delicious food they had ever tasted.' Perhaps one day when we arrive in his country, in heaven, we too will hear Christ say to us, 'Come and have breakfast' as he did to his friends on the shores of Galilee.

Joy-gathering

- How can you contribute to the shared joy of your church or your household? Reflect on what you might do to bring joy to others by engaging with fellowship meals, acts of hospitality, coffee appointments. Perhaps reinstate saying grace before eating.
- Think back over the companions God has given you at different times of your life and how they brought you joy. Give thanks for them.
- Who brought you joy today, even in the simplest of ways? Who rubbed you up the wrong way? Give both to God.

Creation Joy

3

Lewis's celebratory approach to nature can help us open ourselves to a much greater depth of joy in three main ways: by providing powerful metaphors for the new life God has given us; by inspiring deeper worship; and by embodying a glorious vision of the Christian hope.

Lewis developed a very sensitive appreciation of the natural world in his early teens. At first he sought idealized landscapes which could have come from Norse myths, especially Wagner's operatic interpretations of them, but in time he found that 'nature ceased to be a mere reminder of the books, became herself the medium of the real joy.'[23]

Even during his years as a pupil at Malvern College, though he hated much of the life there, the natural world could seem like paradise: 'What keen, tingling sunlight there was! The mere smells were enough to make a man tipsy—cut grass, dew-dabbled mosses, sweet pea, autumn woods, wood burning, peat, salt water. The sense ached. I was sick with desire.'[24] Joy flowed through creation, even in his professed atheist stage.

Symbols of the Kingdom

Underpinning his ideas about the created order is Lewis's principle that the beauties and glories of nature are an image of, and vehicle for, a splendour beyond this world. He points this out many times. This approach to creation encourages us to find there symbols which speak to our own journey into joy. His use of springtime is a prime example, symbolizing a blessed transformation in the soul, most noticeably in *The Lion, The Witch and The Wardrobe*. Here snow seems at first part of the magical charm of Narnia but to the creatures who live there it is a curse, summed up in Mr Tumnus' famous phrase, which comes no less than four times in the story, 'Always winter and never Christmas.'

It is completely silent, for everyone lives in fear in the forest. No bird sings. When the Witch appears on a sleigh with reindeer and red harness and jingling bells it is as a parody of Father Christmas. She is the enemy who comes to steal and destroy, not to give gifts and make merry. Narnia is at first a representation of our lives under a spiritual shadow, without joy. We have all known it.

Only with Aslan the lion, who is like Christ in that world, does spring arrive. His coming into the sterile winter of the tyrannical White Witch is like the incarnation of Christ, bringing with him a new order of things, a new reign of joy and peace and justice, symbolized and enacted by the liberation of the entire created order, much as Paul predicts in Rom 8.21 when 'The creation itself will be set free from its bondage to decay and will obtain the freedom of the glory of the children of God.' In *The Lion, the Witch and the Wardrobe* you see it first through the eyes of Edmund, in one of the loveliest passages of the Narnia series: there was a 'great leap' in the traitor's heart, at things to do with light and flower and song. Previously he had wanted to build roads and railways and pass laws restricting the beavers' dam-building projects, but now he notices the beauty of it all and it is a sign that he is changing. His redemption draws near.

Nature mediates the joy big time in these chapters of the story

Nature mediates the joy big time in these chapters of the story. First comes the music of babbling streams followed by the appearance of glowing spring colours out of the icy white: fresh young larch-green, celandines and crocuses and primroses, and the new gold-green leaves of the beech trees. There are kingfishers, and a blue, blue sky. There is warm sunshine and birdsong and humming of bees. The children exclaim with delight at every wonderful fragrance and sound. Lewis piles up description of the melting river: 'a wonderful, roaring, thundering, yellow flood.'[25] The Witch's cheerless winter is overthrown. Joy erupts in colour and light and melody.

In *Surprised by Joy*, Lewis describes his own boyhood as a great metaphorical freeze which was transformed in an instant in early adolescence: 'This long winter broke up in a single moment…Spring is the inevitable image, but this was not gradual like Nature's springs. It was as if the Arctic itself, all the deep layers of secular ice, should change not in a week nor in an hour, but instantly, into a landscape of grass and primroses and orchards in bloom, deafened with bird songs and astir with running water. I can lay my hand on the very moment.'[26]

The trigger was a specific time in the classroom in 1911 when his 13-year-old eye fell on the words 'Siegfried and the Twilight of the Gods,' a record review of Wagner's opera based on Norse myth, and the illustration by Arthur Rackham which came with it. The 'stabs of joy' he had known as a child began to visit him again. He calls it an 'imaginative Renaissance,' a rebirth.[27] It simultaneously generated a love for the natural world. There is an obvious parallel between this very sudden transformative experience and the way in which the spring so rapidly ousts winter in *The Lion, the Witch and the Wardrobe*.

In *Miracles*, Lewis maintains that 'Nature has all the air of a good thing spoiled' and he quotes Paul on the whole creation being in travail (Rom 8.22), but he goes on to argue that Christianity promises a future redemption or 're-making' not just of God's people but of the entire created order. He examines at length the relationship of Christ's incarnation to the redemption of the earth, using springtime images again, to describe how we receive glimpses of what is ahead.

So for instance the miracle of walking on the water is called a snowdrop, because 'The snowdrops show that we have turned the corner of the year. Summer is coming.' The raising of the dead (of the son of the widow of Nain, of Jairus' daughter, of Lazarus) 'are early flowers—what we call spring flowers. Because they are prophetic, although they really bloom while it is still winter'; that is, they occur while we still live out our lives in this world (acknowledging that it is hard) amid 'frosts and east winds.'[28]

Springtime and other creation metaphors that burst with joy in Lewis's fiction encourage us to look for other symbols in the natural world. Let us ask for eyes to appreciate the earth afresh in this way. What has God to reveal to us?

Inspiring Worship

Unsurprisingly the response of characters like Edmund to their environment is very important in Lewis's stories. In *That Hideous Strength*, the third of his cosmic trilogy, Mark, when we first meet him, is not noticing the beauty of the morning at all as he walks to college in the city of Edgestow. It is a black mark against him from the start.

The response of characters to their environment is very important in Lewis's stories

Mark ill-advisedly goes to work for NICE, the National Institute for Co-ordinated Experiments, locus of evil in the novel. He is drawn deep into its sinister philosophies and destructive impact on the environment. Outside Bracton College they are turning ancient woodland 'into an inferno of mud and noise and steel and concrete.'[29] 'Inferno' as in hell, we assume. The once beautiful River Wynd has been polluted with rubbish and slicks of oil. Quasi-scientific NICE wants to divert the river away from Edgestow altogether, which carries an ominous undertone. What represents life and healing and beauty is to be removed from the community. This speaks pointedly to our own times of course with our pollution of waterways and exploitation of land.

Nevertheless, on a trip to write a report on the delightful ancient village of Cure Hardy, which is to be destroyed under the plans of NICE, there is hope for Mark. His love for his wife Jane has already made him a little more 'sensitive to beauty,' and we are told how lovely he finds the fields, the clouds, the woods, and even the noisy sound of the rooks that seem to be calling, not insignificantly, 'Wake! Wake!' His colleague calls it a 'bloody awful noise,' but for Mark his enjoyment indicates there is a chance that he can one day achieve the spiritual awakening to which he is clearly being called.[30]

Much later, a memory of those cawing rooks is among the solid and wholesome things which draw him back to a sense of reality, helping him escape from the clutches of NICE, and enabling the rescue of his marriage. Against the sourness and crookedness of the institution he is embroiled with, he recovers a sense of what is sweet and straight and 'Normal,' and it was 'all mixed up with Jane and fried eggs and soap and sunlight and the rooks cawing at Cure Hardy and the thought that, somewhere outside, daylight was going on at that moment.'[31] Importantly nature, a memory of nature, helps him choose goodness.

The created order, then, has more than just metaphorical value for Lewis. It can be revelatory and inspirational, if not quite sacramental. In *Letters to Malcolm: Chiefly on Prayer*, he says, 'Any patch of sunlight in a wood will show you something about the sun which you could never get from reading books on astronomy. These pure and spontaneous pleasures are "patches of Godlight" in the woods of our experience.'[32] The spontaneous, unplanned quality of such encounters was important to him. They come on us when we are not looking for them. He is at pains to point out that they come to us via physical *pleasures*. Lewis always affirms the material world; his fictional descriptions of heaven are usually solidly corporeal. He highlights too the purity, the wholesome goodness, of such moments. They are a revelation: 'This sweet air whispers of the country from whence it blows.'[33]

As we pay attention and notice, simple pleasures give opportunity for joy

These pleasurable experiences can easily be turned towards devotion to their creator. Not just thanks and praise, but worshipful adoration. The 'cushiony moss, that coldness and sound and dancing light' of a brook beside the way can be 'shafts of the glory' if we stop to notice it, if we try 'to make every pleasure into a channel of adoration.'[34] A delight in nature can become intentional prayer when we are out and about. As we pay attention and notice, simple pleasures give opportunity for joy. Beginning where you are, Lewis says, is a key principle that he has learned. We find ourselves standing and staring a little with God.

In his theological book *The Four Loves* Lewis declares, 'Say your prayers in a garden early, ignoring steadfastly the dew, the birds and the flowers, and you will come away overwhelmed by its freshness and joy.' He is at pains to point out that the love of nature must never become a god in itself. If we try to make it one, it will go dead on us: 'Go there in order to be overwhelmed and, after a certain age, nine times out of ten nothing will happen to you.'[35] We can however be aware of the possibility, be ready to receive the 'freshness and joy,' the 'shafts of the glory' when they arise in God's wonderful creation. Lewis himself was in the habit of walking in the garden daily before breakfast. Saying our prayers outdoors is something we might all try.

Lewis teaches us to be alert to the mood of scenes in nature. It was the flavour or spirit of a place which enchanted him, and kept his senses busy. This applied to bleak or grim scenes just as much as beautiful ones: 'Overwhelming gaiety, insupportable grandeur, sombre desolation are flung at you...The only imperative that nature utters is, "Look. Listen. Attend."'[36] He wants us to pay attention to everything.

After one walking tour with friends across Exmoor he bemoaned the fact that having trained themselves to notice every detail, on returning to town in the rain, they would have to train themselves to notice nothing! However, in *Surprised by Joy* he tells us how his Oxford friend Jenkin taught him to exult in any weather and any scene, be it a squalid street, a wet wood, a windswept ridge, and to do so with glee.[37] Accordingly Lewis, in the absence of woods and mountains, could notice and enjoy small things, like the twist of a brook or a flower, even on a 'dull' walk.[38] There is joy in the detail.

When joy is offered to us, as it was offered to Mark in *That Hideous Strength*, creation can become a place where we encounter the maker of heaven and earth himself, our great joy-bringer. Look, listen, attend.

Foretastes of the New Earth

One day in their early childhood Lewis's brother Warnie brought into the nursery a toy garden he had created in a biscuit tin lid with bits of moss and twigs and flowers. Lewis said it was his first real experience of beauty, provoking one of his early 'stabs of joy,' and it became an iconic memory for him. He tells how one day aged seven he was standing by a flowering currant bush in the garden of their Belfast home and suddenly remembered it, and he was overwhelmed by the sweetness and longing all over again. He said his ideas of paradise in later life always had something of Warnie's toy garden about them.

Milton's depiction of Eden in *Paradise Lost* greatly influenced Lewis and we see this in the gardens he invents in his stories. Often they are situated on mountains, reminding us also of Dante's *Purgatorio* where the garden on the hill is the last stop before paradise.

The enclosed orchard garden filled with fruit trees of the most heavenly fragrance on a remote mountain in *The Magician's Nephew* directly resembles Milton's Eden. As the breeze in Milton's poem wafts forth all the delicious perfumes of Araby, so Digory and Polly experience 'a heavenly smell, warm and golden, as if from all the most delicious fruits and flowers of the world.'[39] It brings tears to their eyes, it is so beautiful.

The view of distant mountains was a powerful provoker of joy for Lewis, from the sight of the Castlereagh Hills through the nursery window in Belfast, to the far-off Mountains of Mourne seen from the hills above his home. It was the romance of distance which was key in eliciting the exquisite longing, the stab of joy. Hence travelling further into mountains in shining and joyous processions of people and beasts becomes an important element in his evocations of heaven in stories like *The Great Divorce*, *Perelandra* and *The Last Battle*. Most of the *Chronicles* end with a foretaste of heaven one way or another but it is only in *The Last Battle* that the real heaven-Narnia is entered with its summer air and morning freshness and vivid, indescribable fruits. The whole company race joyously ahead to the mountains, there to meet with Aslan.

Lewis's last novel, *Till We Have Faces*, reworks the myth of Psyche and the god Cupid who loves her. Psyche tries to convey to her sister her deep desire to go to the mysterious, god-trodden Grey Mountain, identifying it as 'the place where all the beauty came from.' She says it is 'my country, the place where I ought to have been born. Do you think it all meant nothing, all the longing? The longing for home?'[40] It is parallel to the call of the mountains, the call of joy, the call of Christ which pervaded Lewis's life. All his moments of delight in nature anticipate on some level the joy of the eternal homecoming.

All his moments of delight in nature anticipate the joy of the eternal homecoming

According to his vision our Christian hope of 'a new heaven and a new earth,' as it is termed at the culmination of the Bible (Rev 21.1), finds hints and foretastes in all kinds of passing glimpses which we are privy to throughout our lives. In the stories this is often represented by a sweet fragrance wafting by, a momentary strain of heart breakingly beautiful music, a fleeting vision of light, as when Eustace, Lucy, Edmund and Reepicheep see through the great wave of water at the world's end, through the sun itself, to the high mountains of Aslan's country in *The Voyage of the Dawn Treader*. These faint and tantalizing intimations, Lewis explains in the chapter on heaven in *The Problem of Pain*, are such that when we arrive in Christ's country we will exclaim: Oh of course! 'Here at last is the thing I was made for.'[41]

Lewis put this into fictional form in *The Last Battle* when Jewel the Unicorn cries out as he gallops off towards the hills, 'I have come home at last! This is my real country! I belong here. This is the land I have been looking for all my life, though I never knew it till now...Bree-hee-hee! Come farther up, come farther in!'[42]

It is the place where all the beauty came from.

Joy-gathering

- Take a slow walk outdoors if you can, following Lewis' dictum: 'Look. Listen. Attend.' Breathe deeply. Employ all the senses. Give thanks and praise, but more than these, open your heart to adoration.
- Does anything in nature become a symbol of your own spiritual state or journey? Or of God's saving grace? What are your own patches of Godlight which bring an intimation of what God is like?
- What in creation provokes joy in you? What does it tell you of the life to come?

4

The Invitation to Joy

We need to own our own joy. Lewis proposes that opportunities for joy present themselves as invitations which we can either embrace or let go. When an opportunity for joy is offered, take it!

One day Lewis was travelling by train out through the London suburbs, when he became suddenly enchanted by what he was seeing around him, inside and outside the carriage. In the marvellous essay 'Hedonics' (which means the study of pleasure), he describes what he experienced: the magic of lighted windows and ordinary homely gardens and kitchens, the charm of passing through deep gullies in the evening sunlight, the beguiling silence of stations on the way: 'All these things between them built up for me a degree of happiness which I must not try to assess because, if I did, you would think I was exaggerating.'[43]

He tells us this heady delight did not come automatically. It was offered to him: 'One was invited to surrender to it' and he could choose to receive it or not. Just as real and responsible was the suggestion that he should spend his valuable time thinking about much more mundane things, such as the job he was on his way to do in Harrow, and how irksome the journey home to Oxford would be afterwards. But no, he says, 'I accepted the invitation—threw myself open to this feathery, impalpable, tingling invitation. The rest of the journey I passed in a state which can be described only as joy.'

It is not necessarily easy to open ourselves to spontaneous joy

It is not necessarily easy of course to open ourselves to this kind of spontaneous joy. Many things occupy our minds and distract us, whether it is planning dinner, churning over a difficult conversation, or any larger anxiety, grief or uncertainty which threatens our headspace. It is easy to be blind to the beauty and holiness around us. But even when our minds seem overwhelmed by distractions reasons for joy remain, and so we can still make choices for joy. Lewis's experience on the train teaches us to be on our guard against the things which commonly steal our joy, and stand ready to take delight in the small things.

Pray for eyes to see the moment for joy. Train yourself through practice. Set out each day with an intention to be awake and alive to delight. Some people have a theme for the year; make this intention your theme for whatever season you are in—as I write it is Advent, ideal for joy as we anticipate the birth of the Christ-child, the coming of Emmanuel, God with us!

The Offer of Joy

Our joy as Christians is part of the overflow of the abundant life given to us. As such it has an evangelistic aspect, not as an argument, but as a kind of evidence that is offered to our communities. We are meant to be bringers of joy in a frequently unhappy world. We are witnesses to the joy which is in the heart of the Father.

At the merry dance of liberation across Narnia in *Prince Caspian,* Aslan and his retinue bring a joyous chaos and freedom to the towns of Beruna and Beaversdam. 'Most of the people fled, a few joined them. When they left the town they were a larger and a merrier company.'[44] Merely singing and dancing up the street has been a work of evangelism.

Thus a teacher watching them from her classroom window has a sudden 'stab of joy' and jumps down to join them. A schoolgirl receives an invitation from Aslan: 'You'll stay with us, sweetheart?' to which she replies 'Oh, *may I*? thank you, thank you' and two of Aslan's companions whirl her into their dance.

Not all respond favourably to the invitation. Despite witnessing the sparkling joy and life of the crowd, most reject it and flee. There are plenty in Lewis's fiction who refuse the invitation, and we see this particularly in *The Great Divorce*. This book was published just after World War II had ended and so it makes sense that so much of it brims with joy. Lewis imagines a bus-load of passengers from hell on a kind of daytrip to the outskirts of heaven. The invitation to joy goes out to each of them in turn but few are won over, even here at the very edge of heaven.

The one-time murderer Len, now forgiven and redeemed, is a bright heavenly spirit, his face so joyous it makes the narrator (also a bus passenger) want to dance. Len entreats a ghost who is visiting from hell, 'Only be happy and come with me.'[45] But the ghost thinks he is a good deal better than a murderer and should be treated as such. In his opinion he has always been a decent sort of person and thinks he has a right to enter heaven on his own merits. He will not humble himself to admit his failings. In fact Lewis has shown us this man in the opening section of the novel behaving in a most obnoxious and bullying fashion to other passengers. He is not without fault.

To enter into the joy of Christ we need to humble ourselves and admit our fault. The ghost must give up his idea of himself as a 'decent' person. Len pleads: 'It will be joy going to the mountains' but the embittered ghost will have none of it.[46] He does not understand that turning and casting ourselves on the mercy and grace of God is the only route to joy.

It is a challenge to us to search our own hearts. The first step, Lewis tells us in *Mere Christianity*, talking specifically about pride, is for us to admit that we have a problem. That of course is a very difficult step, but essential. 'If you think you are not conceited, it means you are very conceited indeed.'[47]

Only those who 'hate' their life in this world will enter into life, said Christ. Unless a seed falls into the ground and dies it cannot bear fruit, not least the fruit of joy (John 12.23–5). Even Jesus had to endure the cross to attain the joy that was 'before him' (Heb 12.2).

There is no joy till we give up control

As this is so hard, not many of the characters in *The Great Divorce* make the move. Not many are willing to say, 'Thy will be done.' With few exceptions, they want to remain in control. But there is no joy till we give up control, till we cease trying to manipulate others. Lewis demonstrates this in one character particularly, Frank.

'Here is all joy'

The final, extended vignette in *The Great Divorce* shows us the late Sarah Smith of Golders Green, a nobody in this life, last and least of women, but now first and most glorious of beings in heaven. She is so beautiful and attended with such light and so many dancing attendants, that the narrator seems to mistake her for the Virgin Mary. On earth the abundant life she had in Christ flowed out from her to all she met, human and animal alike. And now in heaven the love and the joy flow from her almost as palpably as a physical substance. The Teacher who comes to instruct our narrator says, 'Already there is joy enough in the little finger of a great saint such as yonder lady to waken all the dead things of the universe into life.'[48] Despite her glory she stoops to kiss without the slightest revulsion the 'cold, damp, shrunken thing' that turns out to be her husband, Frank.

This dwarf-ghost husband is among the visiting bus passengers. He is dominated by a tall, melodramatic alter ego who he holds by a chain and will not let go, like the monkey that will not let go of the banana. The chain is a 'death-line' rather than a life-line.

Frank cannot believe Sarah has been happy all this time in heaven without him. He directs a constant self-pitying kind of blame at her. With merriment dancing in her eyes she proffers him an 'invitation to all joy, singing out of her whole being like a bird's song on an April evening,' which to the narrator seemed completely irresistible.[49] Her joy is itself a sign, just as much as anything she says. But Frank does resist. He must remain at the centre of his own little universe, which entails being central to hers too. He cannot bear to think she does not need him. She points out there can be no such needs in heaven, since she finds all her fulfilment in the love of Christ.

He resents the fact she did not appreciate what he thinks of as his 'unselfish' acts towards her in their marriage—behaviours which were not so much unselfish as manipulatively intended to keep her chief focus on himself. But selfishness is not the path to joy. Ironically he is blind to the fact that it is her selfless and serving attitude which has enabled her own flow of joy. Cultivating a mindset which is not focused on self is a paramount key to joy.

Repeatedly he tries to play the self-pitying emotional blackmail card—you do not understand me—you do not love me—seeking to attract pity and, in effect, choosing misery over joy. He becomes one of those 'who would rather be miserable than have their self-will crossed.' He does not realize that the seed must fall into the ground and die.

Almost, her winsome pleading gets through to him. Her smile could not but elicit joy. She attempts time and again to reach him: 'Dear, no one sends you back. Here is all joy. Everything bids you stay.'[50] Her grace and patience reflect the grace and patience God has shown toward us. In itself that is reason to rejoice! But sadly in the end Frank rejects the invitation to joy.

Holiness

The invitation to joy is also an invitation to holiness. We noted in the first chapter how, when describing his response to George MacDonald's tale *Phantastes*, Lewis suggests a strong connection between holiness and joy. First he defines the new quality he discerned in the story, setting it apart from other woodland romances he had read, as holiness, and in the next breath he describes the joy blowing through it like the wind—an image which immediately alerts us to the presence of the Holy Spirit of course. Three times he called this quality a 'bright shadow' which is a phrase used in the Orthodox church during Lent to describe a combination of joy and sorrow not dissimilar to Lewis's own 'stab of joy.' Lewis found that this light of holiness and joy now fell on the very ordinary stuff of his life. It was no longer a remote thing.[51]

Sarah Smith, trying to win over her husband Frank in *The Great Divorce*, is the highest example in Lewis's fiction of this blend of holiness and joy. She wears love almost as if it were a bright and transcendent garment. She is ablaze with selflessness and lovingkindness and love of Christ—and with joy.

Perhaps the most simultaneously holy and joyous characters in the Narnia stories are Reepicheep the mouse and Lucy. They are linked by their tendency to clap their hands (or paws!) for joy. More seriously, they are both wholeheartedly devoted to Aslan. Reepicheep longs to arrive at Aslan's country in *The Voyage of the Dawn Treader* and strikes me as being like Paul at the moment he said 'My desire is to depart and be with Christ, for that is far better' (Phil 1.23). It could almost be the noble mouse talking, in his desire for Aslan's country: 'This one thing I do: forgetting what lies behind and straining forward to what lies ahead, I press on toward the goal for the prize of the heavenly call of God in Christ Jesus' (Phil 3.13–4). It is a joyous calling, and the Letter to the Philippians foregrounds that joy and rejoicing many times.

Lucy too has a particular intimacy with the lion. *In Prince Caspian*, unable to sleep as the company bivouacs in the woods, she revels in the loneliness and loveliness of the night: the familiar Narnian stars, the wonderful fragrances, a nightingale in full-throated song, pools of moonlight mingling with shadow under beech, oak and birch, and the near-wakefulness of the whole forest. The moon is bright, creating mysterious shadows and glistening on the creek. It is the 'dark sacred night' of Louis Armstrong's song *What a Wonderful World*.

There is a strangeness about the moonlight and shadow. There is a stirring of leaves without wind, the nightingale suddenly hushed. Holiness. Deep gladness.

The following night the moon is again very bright and the forest wilder than it ever looks by day. The trees are swaying, dancing, bowing. Lucy is caught up in their great dance as she passes through. And then 'He was there: the huge Lion, shining white in the moonlight.' She was 'so happy she did not want to speak.'[52] She is called by Aslan to follow him, at the cost of doing so alone if need be, leaving her sister and brothers behind. Just as when the disciples gave up everything to follow Jesus, the invitation to joy involves sacrifice. The joy and the sacrifice are prompted by our time spent in the presence of Christ, similarly to Lucy's encounter with her beloved lion in the woods.

There is a kind of holy purity about joy

There is a kind of holy purity about joy. We see it in these characters, Lucy, Reepicheep, Sarah Smith, and in the guilelessness of the talking animals: think of Mr and Mrs Beaver in *The Lion, the Witch and the Wardrobe*, or even the canine joyousness of the dogs in *The Last Battle* (Lewis loved dogs). The 'bright shadow' falls on the very humble and ordinary.

I find this purity-in-joy infectious in Lewis's writing. It provides a vision such that when I read Paul's instruction 'whatsoever things are just, whatsoever things are pure, whatsoever things are lovely…think on these things' it is given a deeper meaning, and is more readily coloured with joy (Phil 4.8).

In a letter, Lewis comments on a friend's account of a 'lovely priest.' He says 'How little people know who think that holiness is dull. When one meets the real thing (and perhaps, like you, I have met it only once) it is irresistible. If even 10% of the world's population had it, would not the whole world be converted and happy before a year's end?'[53]

Lewis's vision of a world 'converted and happy' is conveyed in glimpses, every so often, of a Narnia happy and at peace. At the end of *The Magician's Nephew*, just before Aslan returns Digory and Polly to their own world, he speaks to the children of 'joy and justice and mercy,' or its absence, in the world. Lewis takes the familiar pairing of justice and mercy ('to act justly and to love mercy' in Micah 6.8, for example) but to it he adds the important element of joy.[54] Justice and mercy and joy. This is society redeemed, our whole culture 'surprised by joy.'

Joy Comes in the Morning

We have seen in our exploration of Lewis's fiction how joy is released even as it is shared, through mealtimes and fostering acts of kindness. In creation we have found symbols loaded with joy, inspiration for adoration, love of wholesome goodness, and pointers to the great hope of heaven. Indeed, cultivating a mindset of hope, looking forward to the morning, however long the night may seem, is needful.

The final scene of *The Great Divorce*, in its imaginative depiction of heaven, is of the sunrise at the end of time. There is a sudden golden brightness and the full heavenly dawn chorus breaks forth. The forest itself breaks forth in song. The narrator cries, 'The morning! The morning!'[55]

All the sunrise images of Scripture come to mind in this promise of the joy to come: the creation of the sun first in Genesis and the stars that sang for joy; the sun which rose on Jacob as he journeyed on from the brook after his night struggle with God; the joy which comes in the morning after a night of weeping in the Psalms; the sun which is 'as a bridegroom coming out of his chamber' in Psalm 19 (one of Lewis's favourites in the King James' Version); the dayspring from on high which is the coming of Christ into our dark world that first Christmas night; the resurrection morning itself and the joy of the disciples; and the eternal morning of the new heaven and earth in Revelation which is no longer the light of the sun but the uncreated light of God himself.

'We are born for infinite happiness,' says one of the characters in *The Great Divorce*. 'We can step into it at any moment.'[56] Joy is available. It takes an availability on our part to receive it. Let us make every effort to step into it, even in the dark of night. It is part of our preparation for the morning.

Joy-gathering

- Write a list of the things you have to rejoice in, however small. What is there to delight in, to be glad about, right now?
- What are the things that most steal your joy? Are there attachments or attitudes of mind which lead you away from joy? Bring them before our gracious, patient, joyous Lord.
- Look for the combination of holiness and joy around you, in people and in your environment. Where do you see it?

Notes

1 C S Lewis, *Surprised by Joy* (London: Geoffrey Bles, 1955) p 23.

2 *ibid*, p 170.

3 W Hooper (ed), *The Collected Letters of C S Lewis Volume 2* (New York: HarperCollins, 2004) p 327, 17 January 1940.

4 *ibid*, p 748, 20 December 1946.

5 *Surprised by Joy*, *op cit*, p 27.

6 C S Lewis, *The Problem of Pain* (London: Collins Fontana, 1975) p 103.

7 W Hooper (ed), *The Collected Letters of C S Lewis Volume 3* (New York: HarperCollins, 2007) p 862, 25 June 1957.

8 C S Lewis, *A Grief Observed* (London: Faber and Faber, 1961) p 31.

9 C S Lewis, *The Horse and his Boy* (London: HarperCollins, 1998) p 232.

10 C S Lewis, *The Lion, the Witch and the Wardrobe* (London: HarperCollins, 1998) p 82.

11 *ibid*, p 95.

12 C S Lewis, *Prince Caspian* (London: HarperCollins, 1998) p 197.

13 *Surprised by Joy*, *op cit* p 38.

14 C S Lewis, *The Voyage of the Dawn Treader* (London: HarperCollins, 1998) p 34.

15 *ibid*, p 35.

16 *ibid*, p 97.

17 *ibid*, p 105.

18 *ibid*, p 101.

19 *Collected Letters Volume 3*, *op cit*, p 1245, 5 March 1961.

20 *The Voyage of the Dawn Treader*, *op cit*, p 150.

21 *ibid*, p 175.

22 *Collected Letters Volume 3*, *op cit*, p 1158, 8 June 1960.

23 *Surprised by Joy*, *op cit*, p 78.

24 *ibid*, p 115.

25 *The Lion, the Witch and the Wardrobe*, *op cit*, p 132.

26 *Surprised by Joy*, *op cit*, p 74.

27 *ibid*, p 78.

28 C S Lewis, *Miracles* (London: Collins Fount, 1980) pp 125, 146.

29 C S Lewis, *That Hideous Strength* (London: HarperCollins, 2005) p 113.

30 *ibid*, p 108.

31 *ibid*, p 414.

32 C S Lewis, *Letters to Malcolm: Chiefly on Prayer* (London: Geoffrey Bles, 1964) p 120.

33 *ibid*, p 118.

34 *ibid*, p 116–117.

35 C S Lewis, *The Four Loves* (London: Collins Fontana, 1963) p 25.

36 *ibid*, p 23.

37 *Surprised by Joy, op cit*, p 189.

38 Walter Hooper (ed), *The Collected Letters of C S Lewis Volume 1* (New York: HarperCollins, 2007) p 905, 15 June 1930.

39 C S Lewis, *The Magicians's Nephew* (London: HarperCollins, 1998) p 176.

40 C S Lewis, *Till We Have Faces* (Glasgow: Collins Fount, 1978) p 84.

41 *The Problem of Pain*, *op cit*, p 134.

42 C S Lewis, *The Last Battle* (London: HarperCollins, 1998) p 207.

43 C S Lewis, 'Hedonics' in W Hooper (ed), *Present Concerns* (London: Collins Fount, 1986) p 52.

44 *op cit*, p 187

45 C S Lewis, *The Great Divorce* (London: Collins Fontana, 1974) p 32.

46 *ibid*, p 34.

47 C S Lewis, *Mere Christianity* (London: Collins Fount, 1981) p 112.

48 *The Great Divorce*, *op cit*, p 99.

49 *ibid*, p 102.

50 *ibid*, p 106.

51 C S Lewis, *Surprised by Joy* (London: Geoffrey Bles, 1955) pp 169–171.

52 C S Lewis, *Prince Caspian* (London: HarperCollins, 1998) pp 133–135.

53 W Hooper (ed), *The Collected Letters of C S Lewis Volume 3* (New York: HarperCollins, 2007) p 351, 1 August 1953.

54 C S Lewis, *The Magician's Nephew* (London: HarperCollins, 1998) p 200.

55 *ibid*, p 117.

56 *ibid*, p 57.